KEEP SMILING THROUGH

THROUGH

Women in the Second World War

Caroline Lang

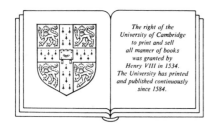

Published by the Press Syndicate of the University of Cambridge
The Pitt Building, Trumpington Street, Cambridge CB2 1RP
40 West 20th Street, New York, NY 10011, USA
10 Stamford Road, Oakleigh, Melbourne 3166, Australia

First published 1989

Printed in Great Britain at the University Press, Cambridge

British Library cataloguing-in-publication data
Lang, Caroline
  Keep smiling through: women in the Second World War. – (Women in history)
1. Great Britain. Women. Social life, 1939–1945
I. Title. II. Series.
941.084′088042

Library of Congress cataloguing-in-publication data
Lang, Caroline
  Keep smiling through: women in the Second World War / Caroline Lang
  – (Women in history)
  1. World War, 1939–45–Women. 2. Women–History–20th century.
I. Title. II. Series.
D810.W.7L34 1989
940.53′15′042–dc19   88-38620
                                        CIP

ISBN 0 521 37747 1

VN

Glossary

Words printed in *italic* in the text appear in the Glossary on page 48.

Acknowledgements

The author and publisher would like to thank the following for permission to reproduce copyright material: Trustees of the Imperial War Museum, London, pages 4, 7, 12, 13, 14, 16, 20, 27, 30, 34, 37, 46; BBC Hulton Picture Library, pages 16, 22, 39; GLC Picture Library, pages 9, 11, 18. Every effort has been made to reach copyright holders; the publishers would be pleased to hear from anyone whose rights they have unwittingly infringed.

Title 'Keep Smiling Through' is taken from *We'll Meet Again*, one of the most popular songs of the war, sung by Vera Lynn.

Cover illustration 'Women of Britain – Come into the Factories!' Government poster to recruit women for wartime factory work (Imperial War Museum)

Oral evidence The members of a local history class held at Little Ilford Adult Educational Centre in Newham, London, 1983, provided many and varied memories used throughout this book. Most of the class had been young women during the war. Their discussions were tape-recorded as an oral history record.

A note on money

Old currency

12d (old pennies) = 1s (shilling)
20s = £1

Modern currency (since 1970)

100p (new pence) = £1

Therefore:

1d = about $\frac{1}{2}$p
6d = 2$\frac{1}{2}$p
1s = 5p
2s = 10p
5s = 25p
10s = 50p

Remember that the value of money was very different in the past. To work out the real value you should compare the wages people received with how much they had to pay for food, rent etc.

Contents

Working on an aircraft: mechanic Doris Bearman (foreground), aged 20, joined the WAAF, the women's branch of the airforce, in 1940.

impossible to move all of them. So official arrangements were made to evacuate certain groups of people as a priority: school children and their teachers, children under five and their mothers, expectant mothers, and blind and handicapped adults.

From early in 1939 mothers living in the danger zones of large cities had been under increasing pressure to consider evacuation if war came, although it was not compulsory. Radio broadcasts, newspapers and posters contrasted the healthy country life their children could enjoy, with the dangers of bombing, life in air-raid shelters and disrupted schooling if they remained at home. It was a difficult decision to make, as one mother from Stirling in Scotland remembers:

> It is hard to think back to those days, but the threat was very real, and the decision to part with our children an agonizing one. We were assailed on all sides with propaganda to persuade parents to send their children to safety. We made up our minds that we must not think of ourselves and our own sacrifices, but of the safety, and possible survival of our children. We said Yes, they should go.
>
> *Oral interview in the 1960s, from B. S. Johnson, The Evacuees, 1968*

When evacuation was finally announced, mothers had only a few hours to prepare for their children to be sent away.

Parting

When the announcement came that the first evacuees were to move out of the cities, mothers were told to pack a change of underclothes, sandwiches and gas masks, attach labels with names and addresses to their children's coats and take them to school. The children could take a favourite toy and a postcard on which to send their address to their parents when they arrived. Parting from children was often a distressing experience:

> The day arrived, and early in the morning I said Goodbye to my two little daughters, Helen and Katharine, dressed in their little kilts and yellow jerseys and clutching their big dolls. I lay in bed and cried all day, and was unable even to feed my new-born baby.
>
> *B. S. Johnson, The Evacuees, 1968*

Most of the official evacuees went during the weekend when war was declared. Altogether 827,000 school children, 524,000 mothers and young children, 13,000 expectant mothers, 7,000 blind and handicapped people, and 103,000 teachers and helpers were moved. About two million others made their own private arrangements to stay with friends, relatives or in hotels in the country, and thousands left for the USA, Canada and Australia if they could afford it. In September 1939 alone, almost one-third of all Britons changed their address.

Billeting

It was an amazing feat of organisation to move so many people in so short a time and understandably there were problems. In some places when hundreds of evacuees poured onto station platforms they were marched into whatever train was waiting, to avoid congestion, which meant that sometimes they arrived at the wrong destination. Even the

9

17.—Clothing.

Besides the clothes which the child would be wearing, and such should include an overcoat or mackintosh, a complete change of clothing should be carried. The following is suggested:—

GIRL.	BOY.
One vest or combinations.	One vest.
One pair of knickers.	One shirt with collar.
One bodice.	One pair of pants.
One petticoat.	One pullover or jersey.
Two pairs of stockings.	One pair of knickers.
Handkerchiefs.	Handkerchiefs.
Slip and blouse.	Two pairs of socks or stockings.
Cardigan.	

Additional for all—

Night attire; Boots or shoes; Comb; Plimsolls; Towel; Soap; Face-cloth; Tooth-brush.

Blankets need not be taken.

Head teachers are at liberty to utilise material during needlework lessons, for the making of clothing, small bags, towels, etc., for the benefit of the children, particularly those whose parents are poor. Such articles, except those sold to pupils or otherwise disposed of to pupils in accordance with regulations, should be regarded as official property.

Extract from an evacuation leaflet circulated in London schools. Children were also requested to carry their gas masks and food for the journey.

best planning could be upset if the wrong group of evacuees arrived. Villages which had been expecting children were horrified when train-loads of mothers and babies, or pregnant women arrived instead, and expectant mothers could sometimes find themselves miles from a maternity hospital.

The way in which evacuees were treated when they arrived depended very much on the billeting officer organising accommodation in each reception area. In some cases *billets* were worked out in advance and evacuees were quickly settled into their new homes. But it was not unusual for evacuees to be inspected on arrival by villagers anxious to pick out suitable lodgers. Many evacuees can vividly remember these 'auction sales':

Villagers stood around watching us as we got out of the bus and went into the school. What followed was like an auction sale. Villagers came in, usually in couples, to choose children. 'Mr and Mrs Jones would like a nice little boy.'

'Which little girl would like to go with Mrs Griffiths?' Nobody wanted the awkward combination of a girl of eleven and such a small boy, from whom I had promised my mother faithfully under no circumstances to be separated. We were left until the very last. The room was almost empty. I sat on my rucksack and cried . . .

B. S. Johnson, The Evacuees, 1968

Mothers with young families and pregnant women were often the most difficult of all to place in suitable billets, as this family from West Ham in East London found:

They unloaded us on the corner of the street, we thought it was all arranged, but it wasn't. The billeting officer walked along knocking on doors and asked if they'd take a family. We were the last to be picked. You couldn't blame them, they didn't have any coloured people there in those days. I stood with my little brother Richard, Mum and the baby. I think we stood there all morning.

Anita Bowers, oral interview, 1983

Anita Bowers was the oldest of four children. Their family were of West Indian origin, and lived in East London. At the outbreak of war she had just left school at the age of 14, to contribute to her family's income. Her father, who had been a seaman, was unable to work because of ill-health. During the war she did a number of local factory jobs, mainly machining and pattern-cutting at Smith's factory, which made military tents and uniforms. The younger children were evacuated earlier with their schools, but quickly returned home. The whole family left when they were bombed out.

In 1945 Anita married her soldier boyfriend when he was about to be posted abroad. After the war they had a daughter, but like so many hasty wartime marriages, they soon separated. Her husband emigrated to Canada. She later remarried and still lives in East London.

Evacuees from London arriving in Ware, Hertfordshire, in September 1939. Official photographs showed smiling school children arriving in the country; in reality they were often tired and bewildered.

Many evacuees went to very different homes from those they were used to; evacuation often mixed people from entirely different backgrounds for the first time. One evacuee recalls:

> At home we lived in a small flat. We had never been in a 'drawing room', never used a 'toilet'. Certainly some unlikely families were formed.
>
> *B. S. Johnson, The Evacuees, 1968*

Coping with evacuation

Once evacuees had been transported to the Reception Zones, it was very much left to the women who were their hosts to deal with them. It was not an easy job. Evacuated children were often disturbed and homesick and it was just as difficult to make a lonely evacuated mother feel at home. Added to these difficulties, many country housewives found themselves short of money, especially when food prices began to rise, because although the government paid a billeting allowance, it was only enough to cover bare essentials.

Some women found it difficult to cope with the behaviour of children very different from their own; others were horrified at the physical condition of the evacuees they had to look after. Many of the evacuees came from the poorest and most crowded parts of major towns and cities, where keeping clean was a tremendous effort because of inadequate water supplies and sanitation. Although many exaggerated horror stories were told about evacuees, it is clear that quite a number of them did have fleas, *impetigo*, headlice and *scabies*. Some were very dirty, some had no proper toilet training, and a few very poor children were even sewn into their ragged clothes.

Undoubtedly it was a shock for those who were better off to come face to face with the extreme poverty that still survived in some inner cities. Their experiences in some cases contributed to a growing feeling that social conditions must be improved once the war was over.

In spite of all the fuss, the effects of evacuation were in fact far from being completely negative, even for those who only stayed a short time. The weather in the autumn of 1939 was exceptionally fine; evacuees who had never been outside the dirty streets of their own city enjoyed country walks, picking blackberries, and playing the kind of games possible only in open spaces. After only a few weeks of fresh air and good food many evacuees, both mothers and children, showed startling improvements in health.

Evacuated mothers

The evacuation of pregnant women and mothers with young children was the least successful part of the government's scheme. Usually only a bedroom was provided, and women were expected to buy and cook their own food or to eat out. It was very difficult to share another woman's kitchen, especially when much of the food available was unfamiliar. Their hostesses were not obliged to share their sitting rooms with evacuees and so some mothers spent their days wandering down strange country lanes to pass the time, exhausted by carrying their small children. Keeping young children quiet and well behaved in someone else's house was also a great strain.

Returning home

By January 1940, four out of ten children evacuated to the country and nine out of ten mothers had returned home. The problems and family disruption caused by evacuation would not have seemed so important if cities had been devastated by bombing as expected at the beginning of the war. When the bombs failed to fall, however, city evacuees were quickly tempted to return home, and their hosts were anxious to return to normal.

It was also very difficult for families separated by evacuation to keep in touch. Travelling was soon restricted and the distances were sometimes considerable:

> I remember my husband, home on leave from the army, cycling from East Ham [London] to Cirencester [Gloucestershire] to visit our daughter. It took him 3 of his 5 days leave to get there and back.
>
> *Oral interview, Newham, London, 1983*

Many families felt that such separation was too high a price to pay, especially when danger did not seem to be imminent. As the Christmas of 1939 approached, more and more children were brought home.

In spite of an extensive publicity campaign for a new evacuation scheme in 1940, very few children were registered for it and only 1 in 50 householders in the reception areas were willing to offer a billet. The previous experience had put both sides off for the time being, until in September 1940, with the beginning of the *Blitz*, a second wave of evacuation began. It was much smaller than the first, despite the bombing.

There were streams of evacuees again in June 1944 when the *V1 flying bombs* began to

Government poster to encourage the evacuation scheme. In spite of posters like this, most mothers brought their children home.

fall, and that autumn and winter because of the *V2 rocket* attacks. Again these evacuees usually returned home within a few weeks. When the end of the war came there were only 54,000 evacuees left who used the official return scheme, and many of those who were left had only stayed away because they had no homes to return to. Contrary to the official policy on evacuation, women on the whole preferred to find any means they could to keep their families and homes together. Despite the horrific scenes and tragic bereavements that many families in danger areas experienced during the bombing, women did their utmost, with one another's help, to keep going as normally as possible.

The 'Bore War'

Despite the initial panic, the bombing did not really start for over a year. Many women remember this period as a most difficult and stressful one. It was referred to at the time as the 'Bore War' and later on as the 'Phoney War'. The strain of waiting for something to happen was very nerve-racking, especially since life had already changed so much.

Daily lives were interfered with in a way that was unknown in peacetime. Many new rules and regulations were announced by the government, and propaganda made it clear that women were expected to play a full part in the war effort.

Air-raid precautions affected every household in Britain; not only did gas masks have to be carried at all times but blacking out became a tedious evening ritual. Lights could have guided enemy planes to their targets at night, so street lighting was put out on 1 September 1939, and people then had to make sure that no light showed from their homes. One woman remembers:

> At first we made curtains with heavy blackout material but the shops soon ran out, so we used black paint on the windows, cardboard, brown paper and drawing pins, anything we could find.
>
> *Oral interview, Newham, London, 1983*

The blackout, which lasted six years, really changed everyday life. It meant that going out

at night was much more difficult, transport was unreliable, cinemas, theatres and dance halls all had to close from time to time. Most of all it made everything seem gloomy and drab. Mass Observation commented:

> I believe the women are bearing the brunt in this home-fronted war. I believe that the way they react to the strain may largely determine the outcome. And I see everywhere . . . very little sign that the woman's point of view matters nearly as much as the man's. This war is being led by men and run by men, mostly old men. They are appallingly ignoring women's problems.
>
> *Mass Observation, Industrial and Personnel Management, 1939*

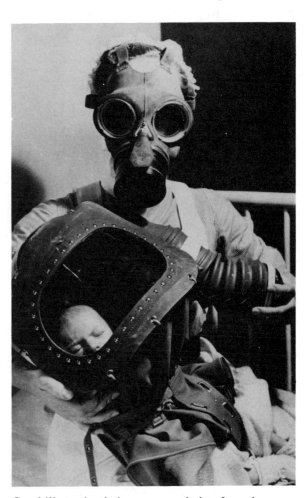

Gas drill at a hospital: nurses even had to fit newborn babies with special gas masks. People were well prepared for gas attacks, as bombs using different kinds of poison gas had been used in the First World War. Everyone had to have a gas mask, but they were never actually needed.

GAS ATTACK

HOW TO PUT ON YOUR GAS MASK

Always keep your gas mask with you – day and night. Learn to put it on quickly. Practise wearing it.

1. Hold your breath.   2. Hold mask in front of face, with thumbs inside straps.
3. Thrust chin well forward into mask, pull straps over head as far as they will go.
4. Run finger round face-piece taking care head-straps are not twisted.

IF THE GAS RATTLES SOUND

1. Hold your breath. Put on mask wherever you are. Close window.

2. If out of doors, take off hat, put on your mask. Turn up collar.

3. Put on gloves or keep hands in pockets. Take cover in nearest building.

IF YOU GET GASSED

BY VAPOUR GAS Keep your gas mask on even if you feel discomfort
If discomfort continues go to First Aid Post

BY LIQUID or BLISTER GAS

1	2	3	4
Dab, but *don't rub* the splash with handkerchief. Then destroy handkerchief.	Rub No. 2 Ointment well into place. *(Buy a 6d. jar now from any chemist).* In emergency chemists supply Bleach Cream free.	If you can't get Ointment or Cream within 5 minutes wash place with soap and warm water	Take off at once any garment splashed with gas.

PRINTED FOR H.M. STATIONERY OFFICE BY FOSH & CROSS LTD., LONDON   (51/504)

1767

Posters and leaflets of this kind bombarded every household at the beginning of the war.

3 The Blitz

At about 5 pm on 7 September 1940, hundreds of German planes arrived over London's East End. The docks and surrounding housing were bombed until 4.30 the next morning. Many people have vivid memories of the first day of the Blitz:

> My husband and I were out shopping on Saturday afternoon in East Ham when the siren went. Well we took no notice of it, but we were pulled into a shelter by a warden. After we'd been down there some time we heard this crash and we were all covered in dust, the whole place absolutely shook. When we came out we couldn't believe our eyes, everywhere was on fire. We tried to walk home but kept being turned back at one street after another where all the houses were on fire. We didn't get home until 8 o'clock that night.
>
> *Oral interview, Newham, London, 1983*

The following extract is from a report made by a Mass Observer in a surface shelter in Stepney, East London, on the first night of the Blitz:

> Already about 35 people have crowded in. Some are sitting on stools or deckchairs, some standing. At 8.15 pm a colossal crash, as if the whole street was collapsing; the shelter itself shaking. Immediately, an ARP helper, a nurse, begins singing lustily, in an attempt to drown out the noise – 'Roll out the barrel . . .' while Mrs S. screams: 'My house! It come on my house! My house is blown to bits!' There are three more tremendous crashes. Women scream and there is a drawing-together physically . . . women huddle together. There is a feeling of breath being held: everyone waiting for more. No more. People stir, shift their positions, make themselves more comfortable.
>
> *Tom Harrisson, Living Through The Blitz, 1976*

A total of 430 people were killed, 16,000 seriously injured and thousands more made homeless on that first night. Miles of warehouses in the docks were destroyed, stores with their contents of paint, timber, rubber, rum and pepper, adding to the blaze and the appalling smoke. This was the start of the Blitz. *Blitzkrieg* means 'lightning war'; the Germans intended to destroy factories, docks, railways and other targets important to Britain's war production, and to terrify civilians. At first they concentrated on London, which was bombed every night, except one, for 76 nights. After the first two months they also turned to industrial centres and ports all over Britain, such as Glasgow, Belfast, Liverpool, Cardiff, Coventry, Bristol, Portsmouth and Southampton. London, however, continued to be the main target. Even peaceful country areas and small towns sometimes suffered when the bombers missed or mistook their target, or unloaded bombs on the way home.

The Blitz lasted from September 1940 to May 1941, and during this time about 43,000 civilians were killed. Seventeen thousand died in later raids. Half of all these deaths were in London. Until as late in the war as September 1942, more civilian men, women and children had been killed than soldiers in action.

Official plans

Preparations made by the authorities to protect civilians proved to be very inadequate. A gigantic daylight attack, including gas bombing, had been expected. It was estimated that thousands of people would be killed. Elaborate plans had been made for mass burials, everyone had been issued with gas masks, and evacuation had been started. *Anderson shelters*, which would protect up to six people from anything but a direct hit, had been delivered to households with gardens. In city centres, surface shelters built of brick and concrete, were designed to protect about 50 people at a time and trench shelters were dug in public parks.

But when the Blitz came it was not at all what had been expected. The bombing raids took place mainly at night and could last for

Anderson shelters being delivered in Islington, London, in February 1939. The shelters then had to be sunk in back gardens.

Women emerging from their Anderson shelter after an air-raid in Lewisham, London. The damage to the houses behind shows how well the shelter withstood the blast.

as long as 12 or 14 hours, and instead of one massive attack they went on night after night. Fewer people were killed than had been expected, but thousands needed shelter, food and clothes. They also needed protection from future raids because more homes had been destroyed than the government had predicted. The areas most heavily bombed were the city centres where housing was poorest and most crowded. For every civilian killed in an air-raid, 35 were made homeless, and by June 1941 over 2 million homes had been damaged or destroyed. The figure went up to 3.5 million by the end of the war. The relief services were quite unprepared for these demands.

Life in the shelter

Anderson shelters were too small for a family to sleep comfortably in and they tended to flood. The communal surface shelters were badly ventilated, cold, dark and damp and had inadequate sanitary provisions. Many had been badly constructed because of a shortage of cement, and they tended to collapse when bombs fell nearby, so people were frightened to use them. There were also shortages of the lining materials used for trench shelters so that these were impossible to keep waterproof and were very cold.

People wanted deep shelters where they felt safe in large numbers. In the first days of the Blitz people all over London bought platform tickets and camped on platforms of underground stations, or in any large, strong basement, deep underground. At first the authorities tried to keep people out of the underground stations, but public shelters were so obviously inadequate that they were quickly forced to give in to public pressure and eventually over 70 stations were regularly used as shelters. They seemed safer than they really were: several were hit, with many casualties. In spite of this people continued to use them because they were warm, dry and well-lit, there were plenty of other people to keep spirits up, and the bombs could not be heard.

The government recognised that improvements were needed. In October 1940 an MP, Ellen Wilkinson, was made responsible for providing first-aid posts, bunks, damp-proofing, heat, light, lavatories, food, as well as entertainment and even libraries in the communal shelters. Official policy changed and the construction of several enormous shelters deep underground was begun. Meanwhile the less safe of the brick surface shelters were demolished. The *Morrison shelter*, a new type of family shelter which could be erected indoors, was also developed.

The scale of damage meant an enormous upheaval for the families involved. Those living in the East End of London, at most risk from the nightly air-raids, began to make daily treks to the West End of London, where the bombing was less severe and shelters were safer and deeper. Preparing food and bedding and setting off for the night was to become a habit for many women. Mass Observation recorded one family's journey on the third night of the Blitz:

> Preparations for the journey began at 1.30 pm. The women had all gathered in Grandmother's kitchen . . . They were to have set off at two, to make sure of getting a place in Dickins and Jones' basement, the big multiple store in Oxford Street [West End] . . . At quarter past three, only Granny and Mrs K were ready. They decided to set off with:

> Granny: folding chair, blanket, slippers, bags of food
> Mrs K: bag of food, blanket
> After some while, they managed to get on to the crowded platform of the underground station – where the rest of the party soon caught them up, with the addition by now of two more neighbouring families . . . All carried bundles. Then the siren went again. The train came in, already packed. The whole party managed to push their way on to it . . . There was hardly room to breathe . . .
> At last the party reached Oxford Circus; as they emerged into Oxford Street, they saw straight away that hundreds upon hundreds of people were already crowding round Dickens and Jones; hundreds more were making for it . . . The Dickins and Jones shelter was opened at 7.05 pm. Only the first 700 people were let in . . . Soon, the entire floor was covered with bodies stretched out on blankets. Some had brought chairs (only small ones allowed), pillows, cushions, eiderdowns, etc. Others sat on chairs which were already there, and on a big round table. Queues formed for refreshments – coffee, cake, buns, etc. – and girls were sent out among the crowd with trays of chocolate and ice-cream. By 10.30 pm hardly any of the 700 were moving about. The heavy drone of hundreds sleeping prevailed, until stilled at 5.30 am when a warden with a loud-hailer shouted from the door: 'All Clear! All Clear!'
> *Tom Harrisson, Living Through The Blitz, 1976*

By October things were already more organised. A Mass Observer reported:

> By 4 pm all the platform and passage space of the underground station is staked out, chiefly with blankets folded in long strips laid against the wall – for the trains are still running and main platforms in full use. On average, one woman or child guards places for six thus marked. When evening came the rest of the family crowded in.
> *Tom Harrisson, Living Through The Blitz, 1976*

Although large shelters, especially in underground stations, became renowned, only a very small proportion of Londoners used them (see table on page 18). This left over half staying in their homes, often in ground floor rooms or under the stairs. Many women preferred to shelter from the raids together, with their children. A woman diarist calmly records:

I was playing draughts with Kenneth in the cupboard. Mrs P . . . was sitting under the stairs knitting and waiting for baby David to go right off to sleep. Suddenly the raid came closer. The draughts flew in all directions as I covered Kenneth . . . We heard a whistle, a bang which shook the house, and an explosion . . . Well, we straightened out, decided draughts and chess were no use under the circumstances, and waited for a lull so that we could have a pot of tea.

Tom Harrisson, Living Through The Blitz, 1976

A survey of air-raid shelters in Central London, November 1939

4%	in underground stations or other large shelters
9%	in public shelters (mostly street-type)
27%	in home shelters (mostly Anderson)
60%	in own homes

Frontline, Ministry of Information Report, 1939

1,400,000 people, or one Londoner in every six, had been made homeless at some time before the main Blitz ended in May 1941. Every time a street was bombed there would be a mass of rubble with gas, water and sewage pipes, telephone and electricity cables severed. There might be queues for water from a temporary stand pipe for several days. Immediate supplies of food were a major problem. If the local grocer or butcher had been hit, women might have to walk miles to find shops and get new ration books.

Hot food was another matter. Some women improvised kitchens with broken woodwork or furniture. Others relied on mobile canteens. These tended to concentrate on cups of tea and there were many complaints that they gave priority to the police, firemen and ARP workers rather than to bombed-out families.

Official rest centres for Blitz victims were used by only about 1 in 7 of the homeless, largely because they were very inadequate. The centres were usually school buildings or

Refreshments for people taking shelter at Holborn underground station. Every night the underground was crowded with people.

halls run by volunteers. The victims had been expected to rest in them for only a few hours, but because the bombing was continuous, large numbers of people in badly bombed areas had to live in them for days. Washing and toilet facilities were inadequate and there were shortages of bedding, first-aid equipment and food. Shelters had not even been considered necessary.

An enormous amount was done by volunteers, who struggled to provide the necessities of life for the thousands of homeless in the early days of the Blitz. Volunteers were often members of organisations like the *Red Cross* and the *Women's Voluntary Service (WVS)*.

Danger seems to have strengthened most families' resolve to stay together and fewer people left London during the Blitz than at the beginning of the war. After the first panic and shock people began to get resigned to life under bombardment:

> We never thought of leaving London, it was a matter of pride.
>
> *Irene Neumark, oral interview, 1983*

Raids outside London

In October 1940, cities and towns outside London began to be attacked as well. Until this happened many people had tended to think that the stories of what was going on in London were exaggerated. Local authorities in other parts of the country had therefore failed to revise their plans and prepare adequately while they still had time. When Coventry was attacked on 14 November 1940 it was the biggest air raid on Britain to that date and much the most concentrated. A total of 554 people were killed and over one-third of the city's houses were left uninhabitable. Many of the surface shelters were destroyed and there was no provision for the homeless.

Sudden and unexpected attacks were a tremendous shock to the population. Experiences were different from in London, as in smaller cities and towns the bombing would affect everyone. The town centre with most of the shops and other services might be virtually destroyed. After a serious blitz in Southampton, for example, all the large

drapers' and clothes shops were burnt, so that homeless people could not get bedding or clothes. There was also a serious shortage of food, the main telephone exchange was hit, and there was no water or gas. At least in London supplies might still be available in another part of the city which had not been hit.

Fear of further raids was often worse, too, because they were so unpredictable. In London, nightly bombing at least made people feel they knew roughly what to expect. In other places fierce blitzes were sometimes repeated for a few nights, sometimes followed by minor raids and sometimes by nothing at all for weeks or even months.

A first reaction was often to leave. Hilde Marchant, a journalist on her way into Coventry the morning after the blitz, met refugees packed into lorries and cars, pushing carts or prams piled high with bedding. Mass Observation reporters found that in Coventry, on the evening after the raid:

> There were more open signs of hysteria, terror, neurosis, observed than during the whole of the previous two months together in all areas. The overwhelmingly dominant feeling on Friday was the feeling of utter helplessness. The tremendous impact of the previous night had left people practically speechless in many cases. On Friday evening [15 November], there were several signs of suppressed panic as darkness approached.
>
> *Mass Observation, Report on Coventry, 1940*

After raids on Plymouth, Devon, in March 1941, people were seen walking about on the edge of Dartmoor with their children rolled up in bedding. Clydebank's population was said to drop from 50,000 to 2,000 overnight after an attack, thousands of people camping on the moors. Some of the larger cities like Birmingham, Manchester and Bristol developed deep public shelters like those in London, at first with similarly awful conditions. But in smaller towns families got used to trekking out to the suburbs or surrounding villages when there was a raid, and returning during the day.

Another reason for trekking was that people could not afford to stay away from their jobs for long and so could not move away altogether. In Coventry the important war factories were back to almost full production within five days of the bombing on 14 November 1940. Fear of unemployment was very real. Some wives in Portsmouth, interviewed by Mass Observation, gave their main reason for staying as their husband's work and welfare.

Taking the strain

Coping with young children, extra war work, dreadful scenes of devastation, separation and bereavement was inevitably very difficult. Lack of sleep was another major problem.

Mass Observation wrote about one family:

Since the raids they have all slept in their Anderson shelter, the mother and child on a mattress, the father on a deckchair with cushions and blankets . . . On the night previous, the mother had spent most of the night trying to keep the child asleep, and had been fairly successful. Even during the worst bangs the child had not completely woken up. The father had wanted to take over her job, but she told him she could sleep while he was at work whereas he would grumble because his work wasn't done properly. As a result, the father had had four or five hours of genuine sleep . . . The mother is the worst affected but makes the best of it. 'I'm lucky, I manage to get an hour or two in the afternoon; not everybody can do that.'

Tom Harrisson, Living Through The Blitz, 1976

After severe bombing raids on Plymouth, May 1941, some of the people whose homes had been destroyed camped out on the outskirts of the town.

A mother of three children commented:

> We can't go on like this, we can't. Last night, I thought, I can't stand this, I'll chance it, you can only die once: so I came in again [from the Anderson shelter in the garden] and went upstairs to bed. But it was no good, I couldn't even doze off, all that noise, and wondering about the kiddies out there, so I came down again. How can we go on, I'm wondering? How can we?
>
> *Tom Harrisson, Living Through The Blitz, 1976*

Many younger women had different reasons for dreading the bombing. These are waitresses' conversations recorded by Mass Observation at Lyons Corner Houses:

> 'Expect us to stay in all evening for an air-raid? I'm not going to. It's awful . . . They've had their time, and now they expect us to stop in every flippin' evening! Some hope . . . down the shelter the minute you get in from work, that's no life, is it?

For the first few days of the London Blitz social life came to a standstill. People left work in the evening to go home to the shelter, and they emerged again in the morning to go to work. At first that was all there was the time or energy for. But as the bombing went on and people became more used to it, social life again became important, even if it was dangerous to go out.

Outside London it was more difficult, because so many people left the town centre at night. Often everything had closed by 8 pm. Even so, Mass Observation found a dance hall in Southampton filled to overflowing with about 3,000 people one Saturday night:

> It was difficult to get inside the door for people jammed in the tiny hall, streaming up and down the stairs . . . The dance hall itself consisted of a large room, with a band on a small platform, crowds of people round the walls, and about 100 dancing. Girls were young, many in jumpers and skirts, sometimes flowers in their hair, heavily made-up, or in afternoon dresses.
>
> The floor was so crowded that most couples just shuffled and hugged.
>
> *Tom Harrisson, Living Through The Blitz, 1976*

Surprisingly, however, few women reached the breaking point that seemed just round the corner. Mothers could not give up, and neither could the many women who had to carry on with demanding jobs or look after elderly relatives. Routines were established because life had to go on, but sometimes the surprising cheerfulness was close to hysteria. Also, surprisingly, there seems to have been little talk of retaliation, according to evidence from Mass Observation.

It is worth remembering that while a major German raid during the Blitz meant 100 tons of bombs, three years later the British were dropping 1,600 tons a night on Germany. One of these attacks virtually destroyed Dresden, an industrial city now in East Germany, where as many as 125,000 people may have died, more than in all Britain's bombed cities put together.

The last, and worst, night of the London Blitz was 10 May 1941. 1,436 people were killed, a record number for any single raid; 1,792 were seriously injured; 2,200 fires blazed for eleven days before they could finally be put out.

The final heavy attack was on Birmingham on 16 May 1941. After this the *Luftwaffe*, the German airforce, moved across Europe to attack Russia, giving Britain's blitzed cities a breathing space. Air-raids continued with greater or lesser intensity for the rest of the war, but were never quite so concentrated again.

4 Wartime shortages

From the beginning of the war women soon noticed changes when they went shopping. Some goods quickly became unobtainable and many others were in short supply. Before the war, 60 per cent of Britain's food had come from abroad, together with raw materials for industry. Supplies soon began to dwindle as the Nazis gained control of most of Europe. This meant that Britain could no longer buy materials from many European countries.

Also, goods which came to Britain from Asia, Australia, Africa and America now had to take much longer routes, in ships which travelled in convoys protected by the navy. As more and more of these convoys were attacked by the enemy, it became increasingly difficult to maintain supplies of raw material like timber, iron, flax and hemp, and foods like meat, cheese, bacon, butter, oranges and bananas. By 1942, Japanese conquests in South-East Asia had also cut off Britain's normal supplies of goods like rice, sugar, tea, rubber, and tin, and food imports were less than half what they had been before the war.

In June 1940, production of many different kinds of goods, which were not essential, ranging from cutlery to toys and jewellery, was reduced by the government. Factories had to switch to making wartime necessities. A new Purchase Tax to help raise money for the war was put on many goods, especially luxuries, making them much more expensive. The tax on beer and cigarettes went up too.

As familiar items became scarce in the shops, their prices rose; wholesale prices rose by an average 50 per cent between 1939 and 1941. Shortages meant long queues outside shops, as well as rocketing prices. The goods which were available were not shared out fairly because some people could afford to pay higher prices. One historian commented that:

> Rich women descended on shops in working-class districts and bought up sugar by the carload if they could.
>
> *Angus Calder, The People's War, 1971*

Organising the family rations was quite a job for Mrs Whitham, a mother of sixteen children.

Food rations

The government quickly began to subsidise food so that prices for staple foodstuffs would be prevented from rising too rapidly. Then in January 1940 food rationing was introduced.

Rationing brought a degree of fairness. Coupons as well as money were needed to buy essential goods that were in short supply. Ration books containing these coupons were issued to everyone. They were in different colours for adults, children, pregnant women, travellers and seamen, who all had slightly different allowances. A woman from London's East End recalls:

> We had to choose particular shops, butcher, grocer, dairy, to go to, then you always had to take your ration book there, because you were registered there, and couldn't shop for rationed goods anywhere else. Shopkeepers then got supplies according to the number of registered customers they had. They always had a few stores to cope with emergencies too.
>
> *Oral interview, Newham, London, 1983*

On the whole rationing was popular because it at least meant that everyone could be sure of getting their share of basic necessities, even if they were not allowed as much as they would like:

> I don't think people realised how frugal it was – they just accepted it. No-one starved. No-one complained after rationing was introduced, at least we knew everyone was in the same boat.
>
> *Oral interview, Newham, London, 1983*

The amounts of food allowed for each person varied at different times during the

Food rationing per person

Item	Weekly allowance*
Bacon or ham	4–8 oz
Cheese	1–8 oz
Butter	1–8 oz
Eggs	$\frac{1}{2}$–4
Milk	$\frac{1}{2}$–2 pints
Tea	2–4 oz
Sugar	8–16 oz
Sweets and chocolate	2–4 oz
National Dried Milk	1 tin (= 4 pints) every 4 weeks
Dried eggs	1 packet (= 12 eggs) every 8 weeks

* *These quantities varied during the war, depending on their availability*

war, according to availability, and some food came on and off ration. The allowance of eggs, milk, cheese, fruit and some other foods also varied at different times of the year.

"I suppose in about thirty years' time people will insist on describing this as the good old days." Cartoon from Punch.

The worst point came in early 1941 when, because of German successes in sinking food convoys, the diet was at its poorest. Later that year, supplies of dried eggs, evaporated milk, concentrated orange juice, canned fish, meats like spam, and other foods began to arrive from the USA, and matters were never quite so desperate again.

Rationing dealt with essential foods, but it soon became obvious that other foods, available in small quantities, were not being distributed fairly. Those with money could buy unrationed tinned foods, for example, at a high price which made them luxuries never seen by ordinary families. So, at the end of 1941, as well as the ration coupons, each person was allowed sixteen 'points' for four weeks; different foods were given a certain number of points according to availability and the sixteen points could be spent as people wished. The range of foods 'on points' increased throughout 1942 and by the end of the year covered dried fruit, rice, sago, tapioca, dried beans and peas, canned fruit, tomatoes and peas, condensed milk, breakfast cereals, syrup, treacle, biscuits, oatflakes and rolled oats. Gas, petrol, electricity, coal, light and water supplies were also rationed. Beer and tobacco, two of the traditional treats for men, were never rationed, although both were often scarce. Beer was watered down and expensive. Bread was not rationed until after the war, although by 1942, the shipping problems made it very difficult to get white bread. Great attempts were made to persuade the public to eat National Wheatmeal Bread instead.

Milk, vitamins and extra rations

In the rationing system, it was recognised that some people had special needs. Children under five, pregnant women and nursing mothers had first choice of any fresh fruit. They also had a pint of milk a day and twice the normal ration of eggs. This, together with two new welfare schemes, did a great deal to improve the health of many mothers and children throughout Britain.

The National Milk Scheme, started in 1940, made sure that pregnant or nursing mothers and young children got a pint of milk, and

children aged 5–16 got half a pint of milk a day. They got this milk at a cheaper price or free if the family had a low income. The Scheme also provided one-third of a pint of milk for schoolchildren.

The Vitamin Welfare Scheme, introduced in 1941, provided cheap or free orange juice (rich in Vitamin C) and cod liver oil (rich in Vitamins A and D) for young children and pregnant women. There was a great deal of advertising to persuade mothers to take up these schemes and to make sure children got their full rations.

In general, the average diet may have actually improved during the war. The variety of food was, of course, much more limited, but people were often eating more healthy food than before.

The Kitchen Front

The way women managed to feed their families became a matter of national importance in wartime. A programme of advertising and propaganda was aimed at persuading women to achieve the difficult goal of saving food while keeping their families healthy and fit. Women found that their kitchens were invaded by the government Ministry of Food. Posters and other propaganda told them:

Food is a munition of war, don't waste it.

To release ships and seamen on the fighting fronts, you on the 'kitchen' front have the job of using these foods to the greatest advantage.

You women at home are winning the war as much as your menfolk in the services. You have stood the blitz, economised and saved; now here is one more way to help and it's up to you. We must eat more potatoes . . . The Government has grown large crops specially because potatoes are a healthy food and because they save shipping space . . .

MEDALS FOR HOUSE-WIVES

THE BRITISH HOUSEWIFE is helping to make a second front — the Kitchen Front — against Hitler. That is why we say "Medals for you, Madam." *Is there anything else you can do?* Read the list of awards below and see how many your household deserves. *More* medals for you, Madam!

A Medal for this . . .
Making delicious dishes from home-grown vegetables, with just a *flavouring* of meat or fish.

A Medal for this . . .
Trying new things — fresh-salted cod for instance — acting on recipes and hints from Kitchen Front Wireless Talks, Food Advice Centres and Ministry of Food Magazine Announcements.

A Medal for this . . .
Saving all bread crusts and crumbs, even the crumbs off plates, drying them in the oven and making crisp rusks or crumbs to use in cooking.

A Medal for this . . .
Never accepting more than the rations ; and going without rather than pay unfairly high prices for foods that may be scarce.

A Medal for this . . .
Serving larger portions of vegetables than usual ; because more are needed to get the same amount of nourishment that used to be had from the scarcer, concentrated kind of foods. Serving three or four different kinds of vegetables at the same meal, and dressing them up with different sauces to get variety.

The Ministry of Food, which controlled rationing, spent enormous sums on advertisements directed at women. Papers and magazines were full of hints and encouragement for housewives.

The Ministry of Food left housewives in no doubt as to what the results of any inefficiency on their part would be. Fines for wasting food were quite high and intended to act as a deterrent to others, as this item in a newspaper shows:

Miss Mary Bridget O'Sullivan . . . was fined a total of ten pounds, with two guineas costs at Barnet today for permitting bread to be wasted. Her servant Miss Domenica Rosa Persi, was fined five shillings for wasting the bread. It was stated that the servant was twice seen throwing bread to the birds in the garden.
Bristol Evening Post, 20 January 1943

Cooking

The Ministry of Food had to try to re-educate women to be aware of the nutritional value of different foods, the importance of a balanced diet, and also to persuade them to use different cooking methods. For example, potatoes peeled and boiled in the traditional way would lose most of their vitamins, so housewives were encouraged to cook them in their skins instead. They were also urged either to steam or to boil green vegetables only lightly to preserve their vitamins, to cook with oatmeal and wholewheat flour, which were healthy and filling, and to eat National Wheatmeal Bread instead of white bread.

Women remember mainly the monotony of cooking, and the effort of trying to be imaginative and persuade their families to eat unfamiliar and often unappetising food. But there were many successful recipes and some strange improvisations. One woman remembers:

One of our favourite recipes, I still make it now sometimes, was corned beef in a sort of Yorkshire pudding, like toad in the hole, but without sausages. We used to put treacle in our tea when we'd run out of sugar.
Anita Bowers, Oral interview, 1983

Dig for Victory

Those lucky enough to have a garden could grow extra food for themselves. The 'Dig for Victory' campaign began right at the beginning of the war and was a great success. There were many more allotments than before the war. Public parks and gardens, tennis clubs, golf courses – even the moat of the Tower of London – provided extra allotments for growing vegetables. Window boxes, tubs on the roof and grass verges in the suburbs produced tomatoes and onions for city dwellers. The most easily grown of all vegetables were potatoes and carrots. The

WOMEN! Farmers can't grow all your vegetables

You must grow your own. Farmers are growing more of the other essential crops — potatoes, corn for your bread, and food for the cows. It's up to *you* to provide the vegetables that are vital to your children's health — especially in winter. Grow all you can. If you don't, they may go short. Turn your garden over to vegetables. Get the older children to help you. If you haven't a garden ask your local council for an allotment. DO IT NOW.

DIG *for Victory*

ISSUED BY THE MINISTRY OF AGRICULTURE

Growing vegetables was yet one more task that women were urged to take on. The Dig for Victory campaign, launched by the Ministry of Agriculture, was the most famous Home Front campaign, bombarding civilians with millions of leaflets on how to grow more food.

Ministry of Food cartoons of Potato Pete and Dr Carrot with their recipes became familiar figures:

> Have potatoes for breakfast to give you energy for the day. Have potatoes for dinner to strengthen your resistance to illness. Have potatoes for supper because they are cheap, wholesome and home-produced. Have potatoes every day because there's always a new way of serving them.

> 'You need lots of protective Vitamin A,' says Dr Carrot. 'Call me in regularly and I'll guard your health'.

Some people also managed to keep chickens, ducks, geese, rabbits, bees, goats and pigs. Eggs, milk or meat produced from these animals could be swapped for all kinds of items that were scarce in the shops as well as providing extra food for the family. There were regulations that prevented anyone keeping more than 20 chickens without handing over some of the eggs, or killing a pig without notifying an inspector, but even a few animals could be very valuable.

One East London woman remembers:

> A neighbour of ours in West Ham kept rabbits and chickens, she used to go out to feed them with a tin bath on her head, right through the bombing. It sounds ridiculous now, but they were so important then.
>
> *Oral interview, Newham, London, 1983*

Utility: clothing and household goods

Rationing of clothes soon followed food rationing. By May 1941, the price of clothing had risen to 175 per cent of pre-war prices and some items were becoming very scarce. Clothes rationing, using coupons, was introduced in June 1941. At first, each person had 66 coupons a year, but this was reduced to 48 by early 1942. Extra allowances were given to some people with special needs, such as teenage children growing fast, and some manual workers. Again most people welcomed the rationing as being fair. The value of the coupons fluctuated, like food prices, at different times.

The clothing industry was producing fewer clothes because many factories had switched to manufacturing more essential war materials. Many of their workers were also called up to join the services or to do other war work. So the government introduced the Utility Scheme to make sure that enough clothing was made at prices people could afford. Ranges of clothes in a limited number of basic patterns were made up using Utility cloth (cloth chosen from a limited selection of standard cloths). Each item was sold with its Utility label 'CC41' (Civilian Clothing 1941). Top fashion designers helped in the scheme and, because Utility cloths and Utility designs were of a high quality, the introduction of these schemes raised standards in clothing. Manufacturers were told exactly what to make and eventually

about four-fifths of all clothing produced was Utility clothing.

With the *Austerity* regulations of 1942, when even greater economies were called for, the number of pleats in a skirt, and of pockets and buttonholes, the width of sleeves, hems, seams and collars were all fixed so as to save cloth. Men were not allowed turn-ups, double cuffs or long socks, and women's skirts became shorter and shorter. Many women took to wearing trousers more often, not only because they were practical for working lives, but also because socks could be worn and precious pairs of stockings saved for special occasions. Stockings were always in short supply:

> I used to persuade my father to draw a seam-line, in black eyebrow pencil, on my leg to look like a stocking before going out for the evening.
> *Oral interview, Newham, London, 1983*

Women were bombarded with encouragement to 'make do and mend', and advice from the Board of Trade's prim housewife, 'Mrs Sew-and-Sew' appeared in women's magazines. She advised women to make children's clothes from old pairs of trousers, baby clothes from skirts, and wedding dresses and curtains from parachute silk. Women kept every scrap of material in case it could be used, and made the best of what was available:

> When I worked at the Co-op all the girls used to do the same – every time there was a rice bag we'd fight over it, because it was linen. In the end, the manager said we'd have it in turns. I made my girls dresses out of them – pillow cases and all sorts of things.
> *Oral interview, Newham, London, 1983*

Other household goods once considered necessities were also in short supply; the government wanted to reduce consumption so that raw materials could be used for war production. Eventually, production of a great variety of articles was brought more or less under the Utility principle. For example, domestic crockery was only made in a small range of styles, in plain white china. Designs for Utility furniture, like the clothes, were often produced by well-known designers, and, although they were simple, the best of them looked very stylish and were of a high quality.

A woollen 'Utility' dress. Eleven coupons were needed to buy a dress like this in 1943. If a woman also bought a winter coat (18 coupons), a dressing gown (8 coupons), and two pairs of knickers (2 coupons each), she would only have 7 coupons left for the rest of the year.

YOU'LL NEVER BE ABLE TO MEND THAT!

MAKE DO AND MEND AND YOU'LL "DO" HIM TOO!

The Squander Bug hates needles and cotton! He wants you to buy new clothes instead of making your old ones last even longer, and saving coupons. Don't listen to him . . . your needle is a weapon of war to-day . . . see that it works full time! With the money saved buy Savings Stamps or Certificates.

Savings Certificates costing 15/- are worth 20/6 in 10 years—increase free of income tax. They can be bought outright, or by instalments with 6d., 2/6 or 5/- Savings Stamps through your Savings Group or Centre or at any Post Office or Trustee Savings Bank. Buy now!

ISSUED BY THE NATIONAL SAVINGS COMMITTEE

The hairy Squander Bug cartoon figure appeared in many advertisements. He incited women to waste money and resources, and wore swastikas to show whose side he was on.

Permits to buy furniture up to a certain number of 'units' were only given to those who were setting up home, or about to have their first children, and bomb victims who had lost their possessions.

The Black Market

The Black Market (the illegal supply of goods) could still provide luxuries for those who could afford them. In spite of great efforts by the government to stop it, millions of pounds worth of goods were sold in this way.

Throughout the war burglaries at depots, warehouses, military bases and canteens provided supplies of all kinds of goods to be sold illegally at high prices. Some farmers could also evade the regulations and supply extra food for the Black Market. It was the wealthy who benefited most from the Black Market. But, with higher wages and fuller employment for some, including women in the better paid industrial jobs and the services, there was money to spend. Although stockings might cost fifteen shillings a pair, which could be half a week's wages, there were always plenty of women prepared to buy them on the Black Market for special occasions.

'Shopworn and Grimy'

An official US pamphlet warned American soldiers arriving in Britain about what they would find, so that they would not offend their hosts:

Britain may look a little shopworn and grimy to you . . . the houses haven't been painted, because factories aren't making paint, they're making planes . . . British taxi cabs look antique because Britain makes tanks for herself and Russia and hasn't time to make new cars. British trains are cold because the power is needed for industry. The trains are unwashed and grimy because men and women are needed for more important work.

Life did become very dreary, particularly for women at home after several years of wartime shortages, with no new household goods or clothes. Rationing also made extra work. Shopping was a constant battle and cooking required an enormous amount of imagination. On top of this, housewives were then expected to spend their spare time making do, mending, or digging for victory.

Although most women accepted these difficulties and made the best of what was available, there was considerable frustration and anger because of the way supplies were organised and irritation at the constant interference in their private household management.

Rationing did not end completely until 1954, almost fifteen years after it had begun, and some of the most severe rationing was not during, but immediately after the war.

5 Women at work

She's the girl that makes the thing that drills the
  hole that holds the spring
That drives the rod that turns the knob that
  works the thingumabob.
She's the girl that makes the thing that holds
  the oil that oils the ring
That makes the shank that moves the crank that
  works the thingumabob.
It's a ticklish sort of job,
Making a thingumabob,
Especially when you don't know what it's for!
But it's the girl that makes the thing that drills
  the hole that holds the spring
That works the thingumabob that makes the
  engine roar.
And it's the girl that makes the thing that holds
  the oil that oils the ring
That works the thingumabob THAT'S GOING
  TO WIN THE WAR
  Popular Song of the Second World War

Women played a very important role in agriculture, industry, the armed services, civil defence and other vital work during the Second World War. Their contribution and spirit of commitment and self-sacrifice is often underestimated. At the beginning of the war, Britain desperately needed to increase production of aeroplanes, tanks, warships, submarines, ammunition, uniforms, parachutes and medical supplies. Increased food production was also necessary. Before the war, 60 per cent of food had come from abroad. More food now had to be produced in Britain as it was dangerous and expensive to import it.

Many men had been conscripted into the fighting services or were working in essential reserved occupations. More labour was therefore needed to maintain wartime production. So women were called upon to fill the gaps in industry and agriculture. The owner of Tate and Lyle's sugar factory in Plaistow, East London, for example, recalled:

The demand for men in the forces and in the armament industries had enabled us to reduce

the number of men . . . quite smoothly. But the call-up programme showed us clearly in the winter of '40 to '41 that we should have to do a great replacement of men by girls. We had no lack of volunteers and the girls did a splendid job and quickly learned to be good process hands and promising mechanics.
  Oliver Lyle, The Plaistow Story, 1960

In this particular factory 771 women were employed in 1940; by 1942 there were 1,222. Although women, particularly working-class women, had always gone out to work, the traditional attitude was that a woman's place was in the home. This began to change rapidly; so did the ideas of what was suitable work for women. These were jobs which before the war would have been done by men and were not considered the usual 'female' type of work.

Conscription of women

At first women were encouraged to volunteer for war work, but it soon became clear that enormous numbers would have to be mobilised. The government decided that all able-bodied people of both sexes would be obliged to take on some form of 'national service', and eventually it very reluctantly announced conscription for women. Britain was the only country at war to do this. Many MPs, including Churchill, were against it because they were worried about the effect it would have on the family. However, there was no alternative. A Mass Observation survey made at that time showed that 97 per cent of women agreed that women should undertake war work.

In 1941, because of the increasing shortage of manpower, the government announced that unmarried women aged between 20 and 30 would be called up for war work. The following year 19-year olds were also conscripted. They were offered a choice between the Auxiliary Services and jobs in

Women working at a lathe on a factory production line. Propaganda notices were used to increase production.

industry. Married women were not called up, but they could volunteer.

Although only young unmarried women were actually conscripted, further measures to control labour followed. By 1943 these covered most women up to the age of 40, and in July 1943 the Minister of Labour announced that all women up to 51 would be registered for employment. Women were classed as 'mobile' or 'immobile'. Immobile women were those whose responsibilities meant that they could not be sent away from home to work, and they included women who were pregnant, had children under 14, or who were caring for the elderly. They also included the wives of servicemen.

These measures were intended to release younger women to work in aircraft or munitions factories, the Land Army, Civil Defence, or the Auxiliary Services, while older 'immobile' women took their places in shops, offices and lighter industries, and jobs close to home. Mobile women could be sent to work wherever they were needed. If a mobile woman refused her transfer she could be formally directed to go; and fined heavily, up to £5 a day, or even eventually imprisoned, if she tried to avoid direction.

As the war went on it became almost impossible for women to avoid war work altogether unless they had heavy family commitments or already had evacuees or war workers billeted on them.

An enormous government propaganda campaign was launched to persuade women to play their part in the war effort; newspapers, magazines, radio broadcasts all urged them not to think of themselves but of their country, and to work to win the war. Propaganda, like this 1941 radio broadcast, appealed to women to come forward:

> Today we are calling all women. Every woman in the country is needed to pull her weight to the utmost . . . to those thousands who have not yet come forward I would say that here and now every one of us are needed. It's no longer a question of what is the most comfortable arrangement for each family. We are fighting for our lives – for our freedom and our future. We are all in it together, and what is already being done by other women you can do. Don't be afraid of being alone in your sacrifice – however great it may be; all round you you will find that your burdens and perplexities are shared. All those little things that are so important in every woman's life – we treasure them and cling to them, they are our life-blood. And now we have got to fight for them. Isn't it worth it? Together, yes it is.
>
> *Diana Thomas, BBC Home Services Broadcast,*
> *May 1941*

The following remarks made by a female member of the Local Council in West Ham, London, were repeated in a local newspaper:

> How astonishing it is how, when the country is in a muddle, women are regarded as very important. This is not the first time. I did a man's job in the last war and enjoyed it. Women should get on with the job, do it well, and ask for the good conditions they are entitled to have.
>
> *West Ham Gazette, 1941*

Women in industry

Manufacturing military supplies was one of the most essential wartime jobs, and thousands of new workers were needed as large numbers of men joined the armed forces. A typical example was the manufacture of bombers. The War Cabinet decided to increase production of bombers in September 1941, and this programme of building required 850,000 extra workers. New factories were often built in remote country areas for security reasons, so labour had to be brought in. Many of the mobile women eligible for conscription were sent to these factories from all over the country, and accommodated in hostels. Local women from surrounding villages were also employed, and local housewives encouraged to work part-time, or to undertake out-work at home.

Propaganda made factory work sound challenging and rewarding, and the life of a factory girl exciting, independent – and even glamorous. There were some women who did skilled work, and earned high rates of pay on the railways, in shipbuilding, aircraft production, and branches of engineering. In many cases they exceeded production targets with amazing stamina and efficiency. But although advertisements might show beautifully manicured women in well-tailored dungarees doing exciting jobs, the reality was rather different for many female industrial workers. Boredom and monotony were the things most factory women complained about. There was also deafening noise, dirt, dangerous equipment, and lack of ventilation and light because of blacked out windows. A sixty-hour week, or even longer, was not unusual.

A Personnel Manager in one factory wrote in his diary:

> They had been told stories of nice clean factories with everything up-to-date and all modern amenities . . . I was seriously concerned myself as our factory is an old shabby place and its sanitary arrangements of a very low standard. Our canteen is not good, . . . Lavatory accommodation such as most factory hands use without a qualm will revolt these girls . . .
>
> *Mass Observation, Puzzled People, 1947*

Although local factory-class girls would be used to such working conditions, he continued, outsiders brought in by conscription would be unhappy.

However Mrs Groves, who had done factory work before, remembers her six years of wartime industrial work as enjoyable ones:

> I was 20 when I was called-up for service. I applied to go into the Land Army, but was told there were too many in that and I would have to go into munitions. I was sent away to Stoke-on-Trent . . . I wasn't very keen at first.
> When we arrived the hostel wasn't finished, but eventually it was the best and anyone special always visited us, like Mrs Roosevelt or the Queen Mother. We shared a double room. It was very well organised with a laundry, hairdressers, shops, games rooms and different

sorts of entertainment; dances, ENSA [Entertainments National Service Association] concerts, bus trips and fetes. The army and navy from local bases used to come to our functions and we went to theirs, the US Army took us on American picnics and Glenn Miller even played once at a dance at their base.

I was very homesick at first, but once you got settled in you didn't really have time to feel lonely because there was so much going on. There were girls from all over the country, Scotland, Ireland, Wales, Lancashire, Yorkshire. In one house were a lot of men from Ireland, they'd come because of the unemployment, but the other 14 houses were mainly for women.

We had a choice of working in the hostel as housemaids, cleaners, hairdressers or in the laundries, shops or canteens or in the factory. In the factory, we were allocated to different sections, the girls that were really A1 were put into the part that made the most dangerous shells and bullets. I was sent to make bullets, small bombs and shells, we used TNT, gelignite and neonite. The work was dangerous, sometimes people got fingers blown off, or it could be more serious, you just got used to it. If you worked with TNT, you'd get a nice rash and also your face and hair would go yellow. The work was always boring, but there was always someone near to you to chat to. There were about 20 people in each workshop, I think there were 14,000 altogether in the factory.

We were picked up by a bus from the hostel and taken to the factory, you had to show a pass to get in. Before going into the workshop, we had to leave all our clothes, shoes, hairclips, cigarettes and matches, everything, one side of a barrier, cross over and put on factory shoes, turbans and flannel suits. The shifts were 7 am to 3 pm, 3 pm to 10 pm; and 10 pm to 6 am. The night shift was the worst. As one shift ended, the next one started, so no time was wasted. Considering the way we worked, the wages weren't all that good. We got about £4. 10s a week, 21 shillings were taken out for our hostel and there was tax and other things. I suppose I had about £2. 10s to spend, but we couldn't go out very far because of the shift work and the hostel was in the middle of fields, so there wasn't much to spend it on. If you worked with TNT that was classed as dangerous and you got an extra shilling a week danger money. It was a bit more than I'd earned before.

Every three weeks you could have a week-end off, from 10 o'clock Friday night to 7 o'clock Monday morning. We had seven days' leave, with a free transport pass, every six months. We were treated just like the Services. I still write to some of the girls. I was away just

on six years but it didn't seem like six years to me.

Oral interview, Mrs Groves, 1983

Mrs Groves was brought up in Forest Gate, London, and had worked at box-making in Yardley's Cosmetic Factory since leaving school when she was 14. She was conscripted in 1940 as a single mobile woman, and was sent to a munitions factory. After the war she returned to her old job, married when she was 29, and today lives in East London with her family.

The Land Army

Back to the land, with its clay and its sand,
Its granite and gravel and grit,
You grow barley and wheat
And potatoes to eat
To make sure that the nation keeps fit . . .
Women's Land Army Song

The Women's Land Army had operated on a smaller scale in the First World War, and was re-formed in June 1939. Land Girls, as the recruits were known, had to be mobile and work wherever they were sent. At first they were volunteers but later recruits were brought in by conscription. They were not really an army as there was no military discipline, but neither did Land Girls have the same privileges as women in the services.

About 80,000 women had joined the Land Army by 1944, to help farmers to increase vital food supplies. By 1943, 70 per cent of food, compared to 40 per cent at the beginning of the war, was home-produced. Although the idea of country life appealed to many of the town girls, and to those who did not like the idea of factory work, life could be extremely tough for them. Pay was low; only 22 shillings a week (increased to 48 shillings in 1944), and they had only 7 days' leave a year, and could work very long hours. Lodgings and entertainment were also less organised than for factory workers or service women because Land Girls were scattered in rural areas.

They did a great variety of jobs. Over a third of Land Girls were employed in gangs who were sent from farm to farm for threshing and ploughing. Some gangs were quite large and the girls lived in hostels: most were employed by individual farmers and lodged with them. One recruit from London recalls:

I was sent to a farm in Essex. There were four of us in a gang assigned to an old steam tractor with a threshing machine behind. Two of us switched the switch over and hooked the sacks on, the other two threw the corn in the bin. It was very hard work. We had to go where the tackle was and sometimes we biked eight miles or so before beginning and eight miles back home at night. Later I planted potatoes, and after a year I changed to Forestry.

The people were very resentful in the country, they didn't make it easy for you, we weren't really welcome. All we had in the Land Army digs were sausages, every day for nine months, she used to cook them in water, they were horrible. We had cheese or apple sandwiches for lunch. We were worse treated than the services; there were no canteens or anything.

Oral interview, Newham, London, 1983

About 1,000 Land Girls were employed as rat catchers:

Rats were a pest in the countryside and the farmers were grateful to us. Our group became really good at catching rats and used to spear them with a pitchfork from across the barn. It was all good fun.

Oral interview, Ursula Isaacs, Women's Land Army recruit, 1984

By about 1942 there was a desperate shortage of timber since imports from overseas had stopped. About 6,000 girls were in the Timber Corps, felling trees, working in sawmills or selecting trees for poles and timber. Women who had trained as workers for the Women's Land Army Timber Corps at Glen Etive, Argyll, held a reunion forty years later, in 1983, and these are some of their memories:

By the early summer of 1942 the Glen was flooded with young women. Early every morning we would climb the hills . . . Divided into working parties some women would fell trees, some would strip and burn the branches, while others worked on transporting the logs downhill, by pony or winch to the sawyer at the lochside.

*

We usually worked a ten-hour day . . . and sometimes from seven in the morning to seven at night. We'd come in from the hills covered in mud.

*

At the time it didn't seem hard because the atmosphere was so good. Most of us came from

Back-breaking winter work: Land Army recruits picking sprouts.

the cities and none of us knew anything about country life of any description. The funny thing was that people up here took us into their homes as if they'd known us all their lives. It became just like another home.

*

It seems incredible now, but the men would get wet-time and we wouldn't. They would finish early if the rain was too heavy and the horses would be taken off the hills because of the mud. But we'd have to carry on until the day's work was done.

*

Apart from the occasional dance to go to the only luxury was a hot bath!

*

For six months I was happily in love with a lad called Will who looked after the timber horses. I never imagined that he'd soon be called up. When he joined the Argyll and Sutherland Highlanders I was desolate. He returned to the Glen in khaki on leave. Then he went to North Africa to his death at Waddi Akarit. It was the spirit of comradeship of the timber girls that carried us through our grief. When the maps we kept of British positions abroad showed that we were losing the war, somehow we managed to find the enthusiasm to work increasingly hard to meet demands. For me the reunion recaptured the unity of 1943.

Land Army Reunion, The Guardian, 1984

The Women's Auxiliary Forces

Each of the military services which recruited men, had a women's branch too. Women could join the women's branch of the army, the *ATS* (Auxiliary Territorial Service), the *WAAF* (Women's Auxiliary Air Force), or the *WRNS* (Women's Royal Navy Service). Nurses were also attached to each branch of the Services. Although they were not sent to fight at the Front, some women, particularly nurses, assisted at very close quarters to the fighting.

Women in the Services did a variety of work, sometimes difficult and dangerous. For example, women in the ATS worked in anti-aircraft batteries, managed search-lights and radar control, did sentry duty, and drove and serviced the trucks and motor cycles used for delivering supplies. Women in the forces were paid the same as men, two shillings a day with food and lodging provided, and were able to undertake training which might well increase

their wages. Courses in the WRNS, for example, trained women to overhaul torpedoes, depth charges and gun circuits, to perform electrical repairs on mine sweepers, to become ship's mechanics, to make new parts for submarines, as well as to use morse code, teleprinting and other branches of communication.

One woman describes her experiences after she volunteered for the WAAF:

I was sent to Bridgnorth in the Midlands for my basic training. How horrible it all was. The truest way to describe service life then was 'spit and polish'. The whole atmosphere was stark and bleak, my uniform fitted like a sack. 'Square bashing' is learning how to march in formation. Very good for discipline. One's appearance was judged for smartness and we were closely scrutinised. I was continually harangued for having my hair too long and wearing too much lipstick.

Eventually, I became a telephonist, being trained by the GPO [General Post Office] in Sheffield. My work was very interesting, but I asked to train as a radio telephonist, which was a much more rewarding occupation. This involved going to Cranwell College for a few months. I there learned the rudiments of radio transmitters, also morse code and how to operate an Aldis lamp [portable lamp used to transmit morse code]. The many girls who sat exams with me came from private schools and universities. Having only elementary schooling, my heart sank, but fortunately I passed all the exams. My posting was to Cottesmore in Rutland, a bomber station. My work was in a watch tower. Three other people shared this job which consisted of four shifts round the clock – so we worked alone with only the duty officer. The work entailed directing aircraft to land and take off. When there was no flying, we had to listen and log all speech on the air waves – especially 'Mayday' calls which were immediately attended to because the plane was usually in dire trouble. The spirit of camaraderie was wonderful, disasters were not dwelt upon. People were so brave, especially the flying crews.

Oral interview, Newham, London, 1983

Women pilots were trained in the *ATA* (Air Transport Auxiliary) to fly newly-completed aircraft from factories to the air bases where they were to be used. As in many other areas, male opposition was at first fierce. The editor of the magazine *The Aeroplane* wrote the following extract about women:

. . . The trouble is that so many of them insist on wanting to do jobs which they are quite incapable of doing. The menace is the woman who thinks that she ought to be flying a high-speed bomber when she really has not the intelligence to scrub the floor of a hospital properly, or who wants to nose around as an Air Raid Warden and yet can't cook her husband's dinner.

But this was in the early days, and as one female pilot remembers:

> By 1941, the shortage of pilots was so acute that they didn't mind if you were a man, woman or a monkey.
>
> Eventually there was no difference between men and women pilots. The women were treated equally with no serious bias against them. And when we got equal pay – that was absolutely phenomenal.
>
> *Lettice Curtis, Forgotten Pilots*

She and her colleagues in the ATA flew Spitfires, Hurricanes, Oxfords, and all kinds of aircraft. They had to learn fast. When she first took up a Hurricane, she remembers:

> I climbed in, turned for the first time to the page headed 'Hurricane' in my new pilot's notes, and looked round the cockpit for the relevant knobs and levers.
>
> *Lettice Curtis, Forgotten Pilots*

During the five years that the ATA existed, there were 153 flying fatalities, among them 14 women pilots.

As the labour shortage intensified volunteers from Commonwealth countries were called for. Nadia Cattouse from Belize, a British colony in Central America, was one of many Caribbean women who volunteered for the ATS:

Pilot Lettice Curtis, climbing into a Spitfire. Air Transport Auxiliary pilots moved the new aircraft from factory to airfield. Nearly 26,500 new aircraft were built in 1944.

From the early 1940s other male members of my family had been leaving Belize. I had an uncle in a forestry unit and cousins in the airforce. In 1943 they eventually asked for volunteers for the ATS. I heard it on the local news at twelve o'clock, and was so eager I jumped on my bike straight away to get to the Drill Hall . . . After a series of medicals and interviews I heard I was one of the first six chosen, I left on a boat for Jamaica in November 1943, where we joined a Jamaican contingent and did six months' basic training. We then left for Britain via the United States. I encountered segregation for the first time when we set foot in Miami. The hotel, booked for us by officials in Jamaica, refused to take us, and we were transferred to another hotel on condition we used the back, elevator, entrance. We were angry, upset and surprised but by the time of the train from Miami to New York we had become very determined girls indeed. Wearing our uniforms with British Honduras shoulder flashes we took our seats normally on the train, although black people were not supposed to do this. When the ticket collector came, we refused to compromise, and helped by a Scottish ATS Officer we insisted we would only move if we were given first-class seats. Eventually officials let us travel in a Pullman coach with luxurious pull-down beds.

We arrived in Britain on a ship packed with US servicemen. I can remember my first impressions of London were in the middle of an air-raid, I couldn't understand how everyone was being so cool about it.

Eventually I went to Edinburgh for special training as a signals operator. We worked in shifts sending and receiving messages by morse key and radio telephones. I was also a part-time PT [physical training] instructor with the ATS.

Oral interview, Nadia Cattouse, 1985

Nadia Cattouse spent 2½ years in the ATS, and then completed her training as a teacher in Glasgow, under a special scheme for ex-servicemen and women. She returned to the West Indies in 1949, but came back in 1957 to study in London, where she still lives and works as an actress.

Civil Defence

Women also did essential work in Civil Defence. They drove ambulances and fire engines, maintained vital communications as telephone operators or dispatch riders, did fire-watching for incendiary bombs, and put out fires before they became serious with stirrup pumps and buckets of sand.

They also worked as *ARP* (Air Raid Precautions) wardens and nurses. One in six wardens were women. Although they did the same job as men, full-timers were paid two-thirds of the male rate of pay. But the vast majority were part-timers, mostly unpaid, many of them women with other jobs or family responsibilities. They often worked very long hours on dangerous work, especially during the Blitz.

Once the warning siren for a bombing raid sounded, ARP wardens, police and fire watchers were officially the only people left above ground. Wardens patrolled their section during alerts, investigated *UXBs*, and called the emergency services if necessary. After a raid a warden might put out a minor fire, rescue people trapped by debris, calm them, provide first aid and take them to the nearest rest-centre. They might also have to deal with looting. Wardens were also supposed to collect any bits of bodies for identification.

Nurses, some of them with only brief emergency training, worked not only in hospitals but in air-raid shelters, rest-centres and emergency first-aid posts. Like the air-raid wardens their job was often frightening. This extract is from a report of a bomb incident, written by a fully trained nurse who helped, with two untrained assistants:

We were then called to a heap of debris (No. 16 was on the gatepost) where a girl was trapped. While taking a short cut with A. and S., S. tripped over a body; this was a female who was decapitated and disembowelled. We helped to put her on a stretcher and then went on to the trapped girl – who was too ill to give her name. Dr S. ordered half a gram of morphine. Hot tea was also given her. The demolition men got debris away as far as her feet and I was able to give her hot water bottles (provided by neighbours). The girl remained conscious, but was in pain and was very brave. As I came out of the hole I noticed the back part of a body in a green skirt under the above girl's trapped legs and told demolition men. The demolition men then unearthed a girl's hand (not the girl in the green skirt) The men made a hole and the girl made noises – I gave them a rubber tube which the girl was able to put in her mouth to help her breathe. Fires started to break out under this debris and the firemen were ordered to keep it down with a gentle flow of water.

Nurse's report, Hampstead at War, Hampstead Borough Council, 1947

Voluntary work

Many women who already had homes and families to run and sometimes jobs too, found time to volunteer their help with evacuation, in rest-centres, canteens, shelters and first-aid posts. They provided vital social and emotional support in areas where official organisation was often lacking. The Women's Voluntary Service was the largest women's voluntary group. They and the Women's Institutes, Townswomen's Guilds, Red Cross and other organisations, filled many gaps,

sorting and distributing clothing, running mobile canteens and laundries, and helping with the evacuation of children.

They also organised a 'Housewife Service' for women to help relief workers in their own streets or nearby. They looked after shock victims in their own houses, helped with first-aid and keeping the wardens' list of residents, and made endless cups of tea. As early as May 1939, an article in a popular magazine showed how large numbers of women were being trained by the WVS in first-aid, ambulance driving, fire-fighting, evacuating children and running canteens, and encouraged others to join them:

At the present moment, women are enrolling with the Women's Voluntary Services at the rate of ten thousand a week . . . anxious to be told what they personally could do to help in the passive defence of the country in the case of war.

Picture Post, May 1939

Warden rescuing a child after a pilotless plane had crashed on a house, June 1944.

6 The effects of war work on women

At the beginning of the Second World War, Britain already had a higher proportion of women at work than almost any other European country. But women's work was still considered to be less important than men's, and many traditional and contradictory attitudes remained.

Women were mainly employed in low paid jobs like domestic, clerical and shop work, unskilled factory work and out-work done at home. Their wage rates were usually about half of those of men and their training and promotion prospects very much poorer. Female employment had expanded between the First and Second World Wars, and one of the reasons for this was because women were cheaper to employ than men. Working women were also less organised in trade unions than men. In 1938, only 14.7 per cent of women employees were in trade unions, compared with 37.8 per cent of men.

Despite the fact that many women worked outside the home, a woman's role was still seen mainly as a mother and homemaker. Married women were not encouraged to work, although in reality many had always had to do so to make ends meet. Even in areas where large numbers of women, both married and single, had always been part of the workforce, like in the Lancashire textile industries, women who left work to have children had no claim to have their old jobs back or access to nursery facilities to help them to return to work. Women in professional jobs like teaching, nursing and the Civil Service were still expected to resign when they married, so although a few women reached the top of their profession, a choice between a family and a career usually had to be made. This meant that there were relatively few women in positions of authority or decision-making and women's issues received little attention. In the last election before the war only nine female MPs were elected, leaving women very under-represented in Parliament.

In spite of all the propaganda, very little thought had been given to women's needs or working conditions in return for the war work they were being asked to do. Although attitudes to women's work had changed through necessity, attitudes to their domestic role had not. In addition they were still treated as second-class workers in terms of pay.

Working mothers and working wives

Although married women were not conscripted, the labour shortage meant that they were under great pressure to volunteer for war work. Many desperately needed the extra income, especially the wives of servicemen, who were very poorly paid. As one soldier's wife remarked:

> You can't afford to keep a child on the army money, so I've got to work.
> *Mass Observation, Speak for Yourself, 1984*

At first there were fewer jobs for women because many of the traditionally 'female' industrial jobs, in areas like textiles, pottery and clothing, were not available as they were not essential to the war effort.

By 1943 it was estimated that 43 per cent of women in paid work were married, about a third of them had children under 14. Factories by now had switched from other work to producing wartime necessities. Clothing manufacturers, for example, might now be making parachutes, and could provide factory work close to home for thousands of immobile workers. There were special problems to be faced by women with families. They were summed up by the Labour Research Department in 1942:

Thousands of women who want to volunteer find it difficult or impossible to undertake a war job. The most important reasons are: low wages, insufficient day nurseries, long working hours and consequent shopping difficulties, bad canteens and inadequate transport.

Working wives were faced with the constant problem of having two jobs, one in the home and the other at work. It was very difficult to fit in cooking, shopping, housework and childcare with the long hours required in a full-time job, particularly at a time when domestic tasks were considered entirely the woman's responsibility. Very few men expected to take much part in childcare or housework.

Childcare

Nurseries were the most pressing need. For a considerable time, the Ministry of Health did nothing, maintaining that there was little real demand for them, but it was forced to take action when women's labour became essential from the end of 1941. Then, all local education authorities were told to provide

nurseries. There had been only fourteen nurseries in the country at the end of 1940; by 1944 there were 1,450. However, in practice they were mainly to enable women to work in a few key areas, and only a small minority of working mothers ever had access to a nursery in wartime. War workers' children who were not at school were usually looked after by relatives, neighbours or some other private arrangement, just as in peacetime.

Shopping

Factory hours made normal shopping impossible. A family's ration book could only be registered at one grocery shop, and by the time a woman got there after work, it would be likely that she would find the usual queues, and also that many of the goods had already been snapped up. Before the war, shops generally opened until fairly late in the evening, but now had been ordered to close early, especially in winter, to save power. Working women found that they had no time to queue for unrationed goods, and might have to shop in the lunch hour, missing their own meal, or on Saturday afternoon when the shops were at their most crowded. This problem contributed to high rates of absenteeism in the factories.

The need for women to have regular time off for shopping in order to combat this was only seriously tackled in the summer of 1942, when the Ministry of Labour called on managements to:

> . . . recognise frankly that many workers, especially women, cannot be expected to work five and a half days a week, for long hours, week in week out, if they have to spend, in addition, two or three hours a day or even more in travelling or if they have homes and young children to look after.
> *The Problem of Absenteeism, HMSO, 1942*

In some factories, women were given time off to do their shopping, or hours were staggered. Elsewhere, shopkeepers gave war workers priority cards to jump queues, and some factories even employed professional shoppers to take women's orders. But generally the problem was never satisfactorily dealt with, and working women were left largely to make

Mothers protesting at the lack of nurseries for young children, in London, 1942. Shortage of nursery provision prevented them from taking up important war work.

arrangements between themselves, just as they did with childcare.

Trade unions

The trade unions became a vital part of the war effort. Important trade union leaders were brought into the government, like Ernest Bevin, leader of the Transport and General Workers' Union, as Minister of Labour. As was usual at times of full employment, trade union membership grew during the war years. The General trade unions recorded increases in their numbers of female members too, and eventually some of the skilled workers' unions were forced to admit women to membership for the first time. In 1943, when the AEU (Amalgamated Engineering Union) first recruited women, nearly 140,000 women joined. The number of women in all trade unions nearly doubled, but even so, the proportion of union membership among female workers remained only about half that of male workers.

Women proved to be quick and easy to train at many jobs which they had rarely or never had the chance to do before. Even jobs which required sheer physical strength were not always beyond housewives used to struggling with shopping baskets and small children. In 1943, 34 per cent of engineering workers were women, 52 per cent of chemical workers, 22 per cent of metal workers, 20 per cent of transport workers and 46 per cent of national and local government workers.

Male workers were concerned by this and saw women as a threat to both jobs and wage levels. There had been unemployment before the war and they suspected that employers might continue to use women to replace them in peacetime because they were paid lower wages. The President of the AEU remarked:

The system which allows women to be brought into industry as 'cheap labour' and uses them with the double object of exploiting them and undermining the men's rates has left its scars on us all.

Wal Hannington, President of the AEU, 1943

This prompted unions to seek arrangements with the government on wages for women,

especially in the skilled, traditionally male sectors of employment. They were really much more concerned with protecting men's jobs than with women's wage rates. Women were seen by them only as a temporary wartime addition to the workforce. In areas where these skilled unions were particularly strong, for example in shipbuilding, foundry work, printing, sheet-metal work and toolmaking, women workers were almost completely removed at the end of the war.

Striking for equal pay

Women were still treated as second class workers and inequality of earnings was taken for granted. Women did relatively well in many wartime jobs compared with their previous peacetime wages, but men still took home much more money for the same work. For instance, women on government training schemes were paid less than two-thirds of the wage of male trainees. This contradictory attitude is shown clearly in this extract from a history of Tate and Lyle's sugar factory in East London:

The mud presses were 'manned' by girls . . . In the can-making Grace Ranger became a near fitter and could clear a jammed Angelus double seamer . . . Gladys and Ivy Lewil could adjust Southall and Smith weighing machines. The catalogue could go on and on.

After discussion with the Union it was agreed that girls doing men's jobs should get three-quarters of the men's rate. This was not so unfair as it sounds. Although girls, for example on the white sugar centrifugals, were apparently completely replacing an equal number of men, when anything went wrong, like a jammed valve or a stuck mixer, men had somehow to be found at great inconvenience to come to the rescue. I don't think the girls felt any sense of grievance.

Oliver Lyle, The Plaistow Story, 1960

Trade unions were concerned to prevent the 'dilution' of many women entering jobs which had previously been done by men, from undercutting male wage levels. In 1940, agreement was reached in the engineering industry that employers could sign on women, on a temporary wartime basis, to do work previously done only by men. After they had worked for 32 weeks women received a full man's rate for the job if they were doing the job without 'special assistance, guidance or supervision'. Similar agreements were reached in other industries too.

But employers got round these agreements by claiming either that jobs had often been done by women before the war; or by changing small details of the job so that it could be called a new type of job; or, most commonly, by saying that because women still needed male help occasionally, for instance in lifting heavy items, they still worked under 'supervision'. A woman shop steward complained in 1941:

> A man is employed to do lifting, maybe only small trays, but this prevents women from earning a man's wages.
> *Raynes Minns, Bombers and Mash, 1980*

The most important war time strike for women's pay was at the Rolls Royce factory at Hillington near Glasgow. By 1943, 20,000 workers were employed, with only 4.5 per cent of skilled men. The AEU claimed that the firm was evading the 1940 agreement over women's pay, and when a settlement was reached in August 1943 it was rejected by the women. 60,000 workers, women and men, were out on strike for a week until a satisfactory agreement on the wider application of men's rates was reached.

This success, unfortunately, did not extend to other female workers. In January, 1944, women in metal-working and engineering earned on average £3 10s a week as compared with £7 for men. The extent to which inequality was still accepted was demonstrated a few months later when women teachers, who quite clearly did exactly the same jobs, for the same hours, and had the same qualifications as men, were refused equal pay. The Prime Minister, Winston Churchill, called their claim 'impertinence'.

Equal compensation

One campaign fought relatively successfully by women during the war years was for equal compensation for injuries, whether through bombing, war service or industrial accidents. At the start of the war, women in the Forces and in Civil Defence were paid between two-thirds and four-fifths of the male rate of compensation, and in the past women had also been given lower compensation than men for industrial injuries. Women felt differently when they were compulsorily called up to jobs with a high risk of injury and there was an outcry. The question of equal pay and compensation was raised by female MPs when the conscription of women was debated in the House of Commons in 1941. Dr Edith Summerskill, a member of the Women's Consultative Committee, wrote of the debate:

> The only organised protest in the Lobby of the House of Commons against it [conscription for women] came from women who demanded that, in the event of conscription becoming law, the Government should undertake to give men and women equal pay for equal work and equal compensation for injuries received as a result of enemy action . . . Although a woman may be called upon to serve and perform the same duties as a man, her monetary value is assessed at four-fifths of her male colleague. If, in the course of her work, she is disabled and loses a limb or an eye, the loss is reckoned as being worth only four-fifths of that of a man. The Government has never explained how a woman earning a living with her hands suffers less than a man through the loss of an arm.

The question was brought up again in 1942, when women opposed doing fire-prevention and fire-fighting duties without equal pay and compensation. The Minister of Home Security, Herbert Morrison, said that he hoped women would not be 'sticky or troublesome' over this issue. Eventually, in 1943, their complaints were recognised and women were given equal rates of compensation. However, the amount paid still varied according to a person's wages, not their injury, so in practice women still usually received less than men.

Working conditions

In terms of working conditions and other health, safety and welfare matters, the influx of women into industry resulted in some improvements which were felt long after most of the women had left, and which benefited all workers. The Government ran training schemes for personnel managers and insisted that larger firms employ them. They reminded managers that, at a time when it was difficult to get enough workers, firms should look after the ones they had to get the most from them. Steps were taken to provide rest rooms, canteens, medical attention and better sanitary arrangements. Women were generally more prepared to take action on their conditions of work than men. Women at the Bifurcated and Tubular Rivet Company in Aylesbury, Buckinghamshire, for instance, all went home during a cold spell, because the works were too cold, causing the management to try and improve the heating.

The effects of war work on women

For some women, war work brought greater independence, the opportunity to train for skilled jobs and take pride in what they did, and also higher earnings than they were used to. Women without family responsibilities, perhaps away from home for the first time, had more freedom. Some women were certainly very glad to escape from boring poorly paid 'female' jobs. Thousands of maids, cooks and nannies who were directed to war work often found their earnings tripled. Many young women, who would never otherwise have had the chance to leave home until they married, revelled in their new found freedom and financial independence. Also for some housewives, especially those whose families had grown up:

> The chance of spending her days outside her own home, of making fresh contacts and seeing fresh people, is occasionally welcomed by such women with something approaching ecstasy, which neither strain nor fatigue can spoil.
>
> *Mass Observation, Journey Home, 1944*

For others, especially those running a home and bringing up a family alone, life could be a nightmare of long factory shifts followed by shopping, cooking and housework. Their health suffered because of tiredness, stress and inadequate, snatched meals.

The deprivation and hardships of the war years had understandably made domesticity seem very attractive to a good many women who welcomed the opportunity of spending more time at home at the end of the war, like this 43-year-old married woman:

Advertisements for tonics, indigestion remedies, and for other war-related ailments were common. This one appeared in Picture Post in February 1940.

> The two jobs of home and work are getting me down. I'm tired . . . What I feel is that, when the war is over, I'll want a good long rest.
>
> *Mass Observation, Speak for Yourself, 1984*

Another factory girl interviewed by Mass Observation said:

> Of course when we get married I shan't want to work; I shall want to stay at home and have children. You can't look at anything you do during the war as what you really mean to do; it's just filling in time till you can live your own life again.
>
> *Mass Observation, Speak for Yourself, 1984*

Some women would have preferred to stay on at work, because they liked the independence:

> When you get up in the morning you feel you go out with something in your bag, and something coming in at the end of the week, and it's nice. It's a taste of independence, and you feel a lot happier for it.
>
> *Mass Observation, Speak for Yourself, 1984*

Others would have preferred to do part-time work, or wanted a change of job. But now other considerations were important; as the war industries closed down everyone was worried about unemployment:

> It's not so much what's going to happen to us, as what's going to happen to the men who come home. Will there be jobs for them?
> *Mass Observation, Speak for Yourself, 1984*

In 1945, when wartime production ground to a halt and the troops started to return, women were quickly released from their wartime jobs. This circular letter, for example, was sent to the employees of Tate and Lyle's sugar factory in London, in 1944:

> The Directors and the management wish to take this opportunity of thanking all employees for the manner in which they have cheerfully carried on . . . during the last $5\frac{1}{2}$ years. The war in Europe has been won and partial demobilisation will begin. Our first duty is to find jobs for those who are returning to us from the Forces. In many cases, a returning man must displace someone, man or girl, who has been holding down the job during the war . . .
> *Letter, 1944, reproduced in Tate and Lyle News, December 1981*

Propaganda that had so successfully manipulated women into wartime jobs now changed direction to persuade them to stay at home. The same broadcasts and magazines that had earlier told them how important it was for them to work now told women how important it was to be at home with their children. Magazines, whether aimed at the housewife or working girl, concentrated on clothes and cosmetics, the 'ideal' home, and the contented, well-fed family and happy husband. There was a successful post-war government campaign to increase the birth rate and there was much discussion of the psychological damage done to children whose mothers went out to work.

However, continuing the trend seen before the war, female employment remained higher in Britain after 1945 than in most other European countries. Some war workers were women who were already at work before the war; women who had always expected to work to make ends meet. War work had meant that good pay and opportunities to advance had suddenly opened to them. The door was now firmly closed in their faces. Within a year of the war ending, more than a million women were laid off or left their wartime jobs. They took second place to men again in the queues at the Labour Exchange, and were forced once again to look mainly for jobs in low-paid, traditionally 'female' occupations.

Women still had a long way to go before equal pay and equal opportunities were practised. But their wartime experiences had certainly led them to have higher expectations and to begin to challenge inequalities at work and in the home. An ex-Land Army Timber Corps worker comments:

> The role of women during wartime should not be forgotten because the output and effort in agriculture and industry greatly contributed to the victory and also began to change male attitudes towards women and work. Although we gave up our jobs when the men returned, the experience gave us confidence, and the gradual progress of women in industry since 1945 must be connected with this self confidence.
> *Land Army Reunion, The Guardian, January 1984*

The changing role envisaged for women at the end of the war is seen in this advertisement from Picture Post, November 1945.

7 Turning the clock back?

By 1945 the population of Britain was in very low spirits after six years of war. With rationing and austerity still at their most severe, life seemed very drab and tedious. Many women found this an especially difficult time. Having kept going because they had to while the war continued, they now found they were exhausted and the psychological effects of bombing, the loss of relatives and friends, separation, fear, and the hard grind of those wartime years really showed. At the end of the war the last evacuated children returned, and demobilisation also meant the gradual return of husbands, fathers, sons and boyfriends.

Living together again

There were difficulties as well as joys in being reunited as a family again, sometimes for the first time in several years. Women had to try to resolve the conflicting claims of children returning from evacuation, whom they were anxious to get to know again; younger children, born during the war, who were perhaps used to having their mother to themselves; and husbands returning from the forces. This extract describes the return of a boy who had been evacuated during the war:

> He'd left home when he was four years old. When he came home he was nine. Alan emerged from the genteel seclusion of his middle-class foster-home and found himself in a place he didn't remember and didn't like. Our flat was small and noisy; there was no lawn to play on, no stairs to climb to the quiet room he'd known. It took him a long time to re-adjust. I mean years.
>
> B. S. Johnson, The Evacuees, 1968

Marriage and divorce

All the members of a family changed as a result of their experiences. After the excitement of the reunion, servicemen sometimes found it hard to settle down in civilian life. Men who had been away often did not realise how hard

Typical of so many who married early in the war, this soldier was posted abroad soon afterwards, and the couple did not meet again for over four years.

life had been in Britain for women left at home.

There had been a record marriage boom in 1939–40, when young couples had married hastily without really knowing one another very well, before being posted abroad.

It was inevitable that many of these couples had difficulties when it came to living together:

> When my husband finally came home, we discovered we were two different people, so much had happened in those years apart . . . I missed going to work and the companionship and intelligent conversation. After a while we settled into some sort of married life, but there were times when I thought that if there was a hell on earth, I was living it.
>
> J. Costello, Love, Sex and War: 1939–45, 1985

Some overcame their difficulties; others were not so lucky and the divorce rate soared in 1945 to twice what it had been in 1930. By 1945 two out of every three petitions were being filed on grounds of adultery. Separation had left women in constant fear that their husbands or boyfriends might never return. It was not surprising that many people snatched whatever opportunities for love and affection presented themselves during the war. Brief love affairs between lonely people and an attitude of 'living for today' had flourished:

> Few of us lived mentally or physically for tomorrow, or even next week. Many relationships were set for as long as the war lasted or the posting arrived for elsewhere. A free and easy, in some ways slightly mad style of living took over. Yet in the background a slight fear hid behind the bravado.
>
> *J. Costello, Love, Sex and War: 1939–45, 1985*

By 1944 there were 1,421,000 troops in Britain, from countries such as the United States, Canada, Australia and New Zealand, who were allies of Britain in the war against Germany. The American *GIs* became symbols of glamour. 'Overpaid, oversexed and over here' was the bitter catch phrase of some British men. *GIs* were very well paid by British army standards, and, with so many men aged between 19 and 40 away, they filled the gap for many young women deprived for so long of much fun and enjoyment. At the end of the war 20,000 British brides followed their American husbands to the United States. Many more women were left behind in Britain, some of them with illegitimate children.

Illegitimate births

The illegitimacy rate almost doubled between 1940 and 1945, to more than one-third of all babies born. Knowledge of contraception, although improving, was still not sufficiently widespread. Abortions at that time were illegal and dangerous. The real illegitimacy figure is undoubtedly even higher than the official one, since the children born to married women were regarded as legitimate unless registered otherwise. One survey (*Ferguson and Fitzgerald, HMSO, 1954*) in Birmingham estimated that during the last two years of the war nearly one-third of all illegitimate births were to married women. Unmarried women with babies were not eligible for maternity benefits at first, and

attitudes were very intolerant. By 1945 they were allowed to have small child support and maternity grants, a concession that the government was forced to agree to in the light of such alarming figures.

Hopes for the future

Mass Observation found in their survey of female factory workers in 1944, that women were confused and doubtful about what life would be like after the war.

> My husband hasn't got a job to come back to, but if he can get a regular job, then I shan't go to work. I'll stay at home and have children. I may go on working for a bit, so as to save towards the children's education. It all comes down to money. If I had money I wouldn't want to work at all.

> I think a lot will leave this country after the war – those that have married Americans and Canadians, and those that have heard about what it's like over there – I know a lot would like to get right out of this country, they think there'll be more freedom over in America and Canada. I should think a lot more will want to go than can get. I'd like to go myself.

The survey found, however, that a large majority of women factory workers looked forward to settling down and making a home after the war. Less than a quarter wanted to continue their present work, although nearly all of them hoped that part-time work would still be available after the war. However, very few were prepared to insist on their right to work, and accepted that returning men would probably take their jobs.

> I don't think things look too good for after the war. A lot of the girls would like to stay on, and the boys will come back and want the jobs. I think it's going to be just as bad as the last time, or even worse.

Changing roles

A difficult adjustment for women to make at the end of the war was the change in the official view of their role. During the war government propaganda had insisted that women should play a full part in the war effort. Their labour was needed in wartime industries and in voluntary welfare organisations; their housekeeping had to be carefully planned and economical; and above all they had to keep cheerful. Women had had a role to play in their own right. With the ending of the war, priorities changed, and women were expected to return to their traditional roles as wives and mothers.

However, the war affected women enormously. The war effort had required their participation and co-operation in every aspect of their lives. Although many felt in need of a good rest, they were also reluctant to give up the gains they had made entirely. There was also a strong feeling that Britain must take steps forward in terms of social welfare. As a shipyard worker commented:

> We must make a peace effort as well as a war effort. We can't go back to the old ways. They're gone forever.
>
> *Archive film used in television documentary, The World at War*

Great social changes did follow soon after the end of the war with the introduction of the *Welfare State*. Changes were also felt by women, for although their wartime independence did not seem to survive after 1945, women now had greater confidence in their abilities.

A woman in her fifties who had worked very actively in the WVS and the Red Cross made these comments in her diary. They sum up the attitude of many women in 1945, glad to be at peace after six years, but not prepared to turn the clock back altogether:

> Arthur [her son] said, 'You have earned a rest. And see you take it'. I shall do, and will turn gladly to reading again, but I must find some outside interest. I can never go back to that harem existence my husband thinks so desirable . . . [18 June 1945]
>
> I felt tired, but ironed my washing, as I'm going out to the [WVS] Centre in the morning. My husband is very sulky about it. He said 'When the war got over, I thought you would always be in at lunch-time'. I said 'Well, you always have a good lunch left'. He said 'Well I like you there always'. No thought as to either my feelings or to any service I could be doing. [28 July 1945]
>
> . . . I used to long to be off and away – could get ready at a moment's notice for any little outing, when I got an invitation. Now I feel I can't be bothered, that peace and quiet are jewels of high price . . . that little simple joys – like my fire, to read in peace, have my big wide windows free of dusty, heavy blackout curtains, see my little green lawn growing free from weeds – content me. War has changed me, more than I realised. [9 August 1945]
>
> *Nella Last's War: A Mother's Diary 1939–45, ed. Broad and Fleming, 1983*

A group of American soldiers and English women celebrate the end of the war in Piccadilly Circus, London, on VJ Day, 15 August 1945. VE Day (marking the Allies' victory in Europe) took place on 8 May 1945. It was over three months later that VJ Day (Allied victory over Japan) was celebrated, and the Second World War officially ended.

Questions

1 Look at the poster on page 12.
   a) Who is the man in the picture and what is his significance?
   b) What is he trying to persuade the woman to do?
   c) Why do you think this poster was produced?
   d) How effective is this poster as propaganda?
   e) Compare this poster with other examples of propaganda in the book. Which is most successful and why?

2 The year is 1945. The government is trying to persuade women to give up their jobs and return to the home. First look at the other posters in the book and then design a government poster for this purpose.

3 Identify the types of primary sources used by the author to write this book. Are some sources more useful to the historian than others? Give reasons for your answer.

4 If you were producing a television documentary on the lives of ordinary people in the Second World War, what kinds of sources would you use and why?

5 People talking about their experiences during the war formed the starting point of this book. With a partner, make up some questions that you could ask a person aged over sixty about their life in the war. If you can, interview them, write up your findings, and discuss them in class. Did your questions work? Could they be improved upon? If so, how?

6 How do you think the following people might have felt about evacuation:
   a) a young child from a city?
   b) a mother from a city?
   c) a woman receiving evacuees?
   d) a child in a family receiving evacuees?
   e) a government official?

7 Using material in this book, compare and contrast the differing experiences of an unmarried woman working on a farm to an unmarried woman working in a munitions factory. You need to think about their working lives, home lives and social lives.

8 In pairs (or small groups) look in detail at one of the following areas: evacuation life during the Blitz, rationing, working in the Land Army, working in a factory, or working in one of the auxiliary forces. Prepare a short interview in which one of you acts as the interviewer, the other the interviewee. Write up your results and report them back to the class.

9 Look at the song on page 29.
   a) What is this song describing?
   b) How does this song reflect contemporary attitudes towards women?
   c) Why do you think this song was so popular?

10 How had women's lives changed between 1939 and 1945? In what ways had women's lives remained the same?

11 War had opened up people's eyes to many social problems. From your further reading, find out ways in which the government after 1945 tried to make life better for the ordinary person.

12 In your opinion, did women's work during the Second World War help or hinder their demand for equality? Give reasons for your answer.

13 To what extent was the campaign for equal pay during the war successful? Use the sources to explain your answer.

Glossary

Anderson shelter air-raid shelter for up to six people, made of curved sheets of corrugated steel, designed to be erected in the garden

ARP Air Raid Precautions

ATA Air Transport Auxiliary

ATS Auxiliary Territorial Service – the women's branch of the army

Austerity government policy to reduce the availability of luxuries and consumer goods

billet a place providing lodging and food for soldiers, evacuees etc.

Blitz the night-time bombing on Britain by the German airforce in 1940–41

conscription compulsory enrolment for military service

D-day the invasion of Europe by the Allies on 6 June 1944

evacuation removal of people from a dangerous area to a safe place

GI a soldier in the US army (abbreviation of Government Issue)

impetigo a contagious skin disease

Morrison shelter an air-raid shelter designed like a table with a steel plate on top and wire mesh sides, to be erected indoors

Red Cross international organisation which provides medical care for war casualties, and relief to victims of disasters

scabies a contagious skin disease

UXB unexploded bomb, often with a delayed action fuse

V1 flying bomb (also called a doodlebug or buzz bomb) a pilotless plane with an explosive warhead

V2 rocket a type of rocket containing large amounts of explosives, launched from Northern France in the last months of the war

WAAF Women's Auxiliary Air Force – the women's branch of the airforce

Welfare State a system in which the government takes chief responsibility for providing social security for the population e.g. unemployment and sickness benefits

WRNS Women's Royal Navy Service – the women's branch of the navy

WVS Women's Voluntary Service

Further reading

Vera Brittain, *England's Hour*, Futura, 1981

R. Broad and S. Fleming (eds.), *Nella Last's War, A Mother's Diary 1939–45*, Sphere, 1983

Angus Calder, *The People's War, Britain 1939–45*, Granada, 1971

Angus Calder and Dorothy Sheridan (eds.), *Speak for Yourself: a Mass Observation Anthology, 1937–49*, Jonathan Cape, 1984

John Costello, *Love, Sex and War: Changing Values 1939–45*, Collins, 1985

E. L. Curtis, *Forgotten Pilots* (available from the author, 54 London Road, Twyford, Berkshire RG10 9EU)

Constantine Fitzgibbon, *The Blitz*, 1957

Tom Harrisson, *Living Through the Blitz*, 1976

B. S. Johnson (ed.), *The Evacuees*, 1968

Norman Longmate, *How We Lived Then*, Hutchinson, 1971

Joanna Mack and Steve Humphries, *The Making of Modern London 1939–45: London at War*, Sidgwick & Jackson, 1985

Raynes Minns, *Bombers & Mash: The domestic Front, 1939–45*, Virago, 1980

Vita Sackville-West, *The Women's Land Army*, Michael Joseph, 1944

Pam Schweitzer, Lorraine Hilton and Jane Moss (eds.), *What Did You Do In the War, Mum?*, Age Exchange, 1985

Mary Lee Settle, *All The Brave Promises: Memories of Aircraft Woman Second Class 2146391*, Pandora, 1984

John Stevenson, *British Society 1914–45*, Penguin, 1984

Penny Summerfield, *Women Workers in The Second World War*, Croom Helm, 1984

A. J. P. Taylor, *English History 1914–45*, 1965